JOHN PERKINS

Books in the Today's Heroes Series

A.C. Green
Andre Dawson
Becky Tirabassi
Ben Carson
Billy Graham
Chuck Colson
Colin Powell
Dave Dravecky
Dave Johnson
David Robinson
Dennis Byrd
Heather Whitestone
John Perkins
Joni's Story
Kay James

JOHN PERKINS

by W. Terry Whalin

ZondervanPublishingHouse

Grand Rapids, Michigan

A Division of HarperCollinsPublishers

John Perkins
Copyright © 1996 by W. Terry Whalin

Requests for information should be addressed to:

ZondervanPublishingHouse
Grand Rapids, Michigan 49530

Library of Congress Cataloging-in-Publication Data

Whalin, Terry.
   John Perkins / W. Terry Whalin.
      p. cm.
   Summary: Biography of the African American civil rights worker who
rose from being the victim of racial prejudice in Mendenhall, Mississippi,
to become the head of Voice of Calvary Ministries.
   ISBN: 0-310-20208-6
   1. Perkins, John, 1930– —Juvenile literature. 2. Afro–Americans—
Mississippi—Biography—Juvenile literature. 3. Civil rights workers—
Mississippi—Biography—Juvenile literature. 4. Voice of Calvary
Ministries (U.S.) —Biography—Juvenile literature. 5. Afro–
Americans—Civil rights—Mississippi—Juvenile literature.
6. Mississippi—Race relations—Juvenile literature. 7. Civil rights
movements—Mississippi—History—20th centure—Juvenile literature.
[1. Perkins, John, 1930– . 2. Voice of Calvary Ministries (U.S.)—
Biography. 3. Afro–Americans—Biography. 4. Civil rights workers.
5. Afro–Americans—Civil rights.] I. Title. II. Series.
E185.97.P48W43   1996
280'.4'092—dc 20   96-1034
[B]   CIP
                                                        AC

Interior illustrations by Gloria Oostema

Printed in the United States of America

---

96 97 98 99 00 01 02 03/❖ DH/ 10 9 8 7 6 5 4 3 2 1

Contents

Chronology of Events   7
1. Cotton Picking   9
2. Losing Daddy   14
3. Bootleggers   20
4. No More School   23
5. Tail Kicking   29
6. Cheated!   33
7. Bargaining   37
8. The Shooting   42
9. Strike!   50
10. Vera Mae   54
11. The Ladder of Success   60
12. Sunday School   64
13. Prison Camp   68
14. God's Will   73
15. Polio   78
16. Voter Registration   82
17. Arrested!   89
18. Beaten   100
19. Flood!   110
20. Harambee   116
21. A Dream That Lasts   122

Chronology of Events

June 16, 1930. John M. Perkins is born in New Hebron, Mississippi.

1946. Shortly after returning a decorated soldier from World War II, Clyde Perkins is shot by a white Marshal in Mississippi.

June 14, 1951. John marries Vera Mae Buckley.

1951 to 1952. John serves eighteen months in the army in Okinawa, Japan.

October 1957. John comes to a strong faith in Jesus Christ while living in southern California.

June 1961. The Perkins family moves back to Mendenhall, Mississippi and begins the Berean Bible Church and Voice of Calvary Ministries.

February 7, 1970. John Perkins is beaten and almost killed in the Brandon, Mississippi jail.

Summer 1972. John and Vera Mae Perkins move

to Jackson, Mississippi and begin the Voice of Calvary Ministries Jackson.

1980. John Perkins and his sons, Spencer and Derek, travel to Kenya, Africa.

January 1982. John and Vera Mae move to Pasadena, California and begin the Harambee Christian Family Center.

Spring 1992. John Perkins launches *Urban Family* magazine.

September 1995. The Harambee Preparatory School opens in Pasadena, California, with twenty-one students.

1

Cotton Picking

"Tupey, time to get up," Grandma called. Tupey was Grandma's nickname for John Perkins. The four-year-old boy slowly rolled over and opened his eyes. Outside, the sun had yet to appear over the flat Mississippi cotton fields, but the family was already up and moving about.

"Wake up, Rosie Lee!" John shook the girl who shared his rough cotton mattress. "It's time for breakfast!"

His cousin opened her eyes and yawned widely. "You go away, Tupey," she said sleepily.

9

John was wide awake now, his nose already picking up the scent of freshly baked cornbread and flour gravy. His stomach growled at the thought of breakfast. "Beat you to the table," John called to Rosie Lee. He hurried outside to wash up.

Grandma's little house stood on a hill overlooking the town of New Hebron, Mississippi. It was 1934, and John had lived with Grandma Babe Perkins ever since his mother died when he was a baby. His father, "Jap" Perkins, had left John and his brother, Clyde, to be raised by his mother and sisters. This small house was the only home John had ever known.

On the porch, John splashed water on his face and hands. Rubbing the water from his eyes, he gazed out over the rows of cotton. Soon he would be out there, working with the rest of the family.

A loud voice called from the doorway, "Tupey, come to breakfast or you'll miss it."

John hurried into the house. This was no idle threat! Food didn't last long around the Perkins household. He slid onto the wooden bench beside Rosie Lee and watched as Grandma spooned cornbread and gravy into metal bowls. Grandma served his uncles first, then his aunts, and finally Rosie Lee, John, and the other young cousins.

Almost every day, the routine was the same. After the meal, the Perkinses slipped cloth sacks over their shoulders and hurried off to the cotton fields.

By the time the sun peeked over the horizon, John was already stuffing the snowy pieces of cotton into his sack. He stayed in a row all day, trying to keep up with his cousin, Rosie Lee.

"I'm faster than you are!" he called.

"No, you're not!" Rosie Lee argued.

And they bent over and picked faster and faster, until they fell over their own feet, giggling.

Grandma Perkins didn't own these fields. Instead, the Perkins family worked as sharecroppers on the land. They paid the rent for their cabin with part of the crop.

The Perkins family was known for hard work. When others rested after picking a sack of cotton, they kept working. On a good day, the adults would fill their sacks with sixty or seventy pounds of cotton by 9:00 in the morning.

"Tupey, we need some water," Aunt Ethel called, cupping her hand at her mouth so that John could hear from across the field. "Run on over to the well, okay?"

John loved to fetch water. As quickly as his short legs would carry him, he bounded through the fields toward the well. Along the way, he waved to some of the pickers who dotted the landscape.

John leaned over the mouth of the well, enjoying the coolness that came from the deep hole. Then he lowered his bucket into the well. It took every bit of his strength to pull a full bucket of water to the top without spilling, but he did it.

Carefully, he poured the water into another bucket. Then he carried it across the fields to his aunt, moving slowly so he wouldn't spill.

"Good boy, John," Aunt Ethel said. "That sure was quick work." She scooped a dipper full of water and drank thirstily. Then she passed the dipper over to Uncle Bud, who took a big mouthful, spilling some down his chin and onto the front of his sweat-drenched shirt.

John watched, smiling proudly. After taking a drink himself, he ran back to his row, shouldered his sack, and began to pick cotton again.

Finally, at lunch, the family took an hour break. They walked the short distance back to the house. For lunch, they filled up on peas, okra, greens, and corn-bread. Then they rested in the cool shade of the porch before returning to the fields.

"Clyde, you and John go water the mules," Uncle Bud said.

Clyde, who was thirteen, took one mule, and John took the other. They led the tired animals through the fields to a nearby stream.

As the mules drank, Clyde got an idea. "Let's take a swim, Tupey!" he said. "Last one in the water doesn't have a daddy!"

He ran down the riverbank and before John could move, dove into the water.

John stood on the bank of the stream, Clyde's words echoing in his mind.

Last one in doesn't have a daddy. John's father wasn't around, but he knew he had one. Even though his mother was dead, his father was still alive. Somewhere.

One day, I'll go live with my daddy, John thought. *He's going to come back for me.*

Losing Daddy

One night as he lay in bed, John overheard the adults talking in another room.

John could hear Aunt Ethel's voice through the thin walls. "In town the other day, I heard that Jap is coming back tonight for a visit."

"Well, for goodness sakes, Ethel, don't say anything to Tupey," Grandma Perkins warned. "The boy keeps asking for his daddy. If for some reason Jap doesn't come, Tupey's heart would break."

My daddy, John thought. *I finally get to see my daddy!*

He was so excited that he couldn't sleep. From his bed, John watched the flames in the fireplace and let

14

his imagination wander. *What will Daddy look like? Won't Daddy think I've grown so big and tall? I'll see my daddy tonight. We'll make plans and go off together. Things are going to be different from now on.*

John tried to picture his father, but he couldn't remember what Jap looked like. His thoughts were racing, but he lay still on the rough cotton mattress as Rosie Lee breathed deeply beside him.

In the other room, the adults continued to gossip and tell stories. Although he wanted to stay awake for his father, John was soon lulled to sleep by their hushed voices.

During the night, John felt strong arms lifting him gently from the mattress. In the soft glow of a lamp, John's eyes fluttered open. For the first time in his life, he looked into the face of his daddy.

Warm, dark eyes stared back at him. Then Jap's mouth broke into a big grin. Laughing, Jap pulled John close and gave him a big hug.

John had a flood of emotions. At first he felt embarrassed. *Put me down!* John thought. No grown man had ever held John like a baby. His aunts and Grandma Perkins had held him. But a man? Never.

Then John felt a new emotion — love.

"My, you're a big boy," Jap Perkins said softly. "A big baby." John smiled at his father. Gently, the big man tucked him back into bed.

The next morning, Jap took some time to talk with his son. Again, to John's embarrassment, his father kept calling him "Baby." In some ways, the name fit, because John was the youngest Perkins. So John didn't let it bother him too much. He was happy enough just to have his father home.

After lunch, Jap set John on his knee. "Baby," he said, "your daddy's got to go now."

John threw his arms around Jap's neck. "No, Daddy!" he cried. "Take me, too!"

Jap gently loosened John's grip. Then he stood up, slung his coat over his shoulder, and headed out the door.

John followed his father down the road and through the cotton fields. For a long time, he trotted along silently. But, finally, he couldn't hold back any longer.

"Daddy!" John yelled.

Jap turned around. A look of surprise crossed his face when he saw his son. "Go back. Go back home, Baby," he said sternly. Then he turned around and kept walking toward town.

Not easily put off, John continued following his father. After a few more minutes, Jap noticed his son hadn't turned back.

"Come here, John," Jap said. He dug into his pocket, found some change, and dropped it into John's hand. "Go get yourself some candy." He turned and continued walking across the field.

Jap thought he had done all he needed to do for his son, but it wasn't enough for John. Earlier that day, John had found love in those strong arms of his daddy. He just couldn't watch him walk out of his life.

Jap turned onto a small path and headed toward the Illinois Central Railroad tracks near the Perkins's home. As his father walked along the tracks, John continued following only a few steps behind.

"I must do something to keep him from following," Jap muttered to himself. He broke off a small tree branch and quickly shaped it into a whipping switch. When John got too close, Jap reached out and swatted him.

John jumped back and kept just out of range. He continued following his father. *Why did he hit me with the switch?* John cried to himself. *I'm going with him. I love him.*

John's little legs continued to pump down the railroad tracks. *I've got to be with Daddy.* Tears welled up in John's eyes. He measured the distance from his dad — far enough to avoid the switch but near enough to keep sight of him. He kept walking.

Finally, John yelled out, "Daddy! Please, Daddy. Take me home with you. Don't leave me again."

Jap stopped in his tracks. He looked confused and sad as he stared at his small son. The switch hung limp

in his hand. He just stood there and didn't say anything. After a few minutes, he turned and continued walking. John sobbed as he watched his father stride down the tracks.

Suddenly, John felt a hand on his shoulder. It was Aunt Ethel. She had seen Jap walking across the pasture and little John running after him. She took John's small hand and dragged him back toward the cabin.

As Ethel pulled his arm, John glanced back down the tracks. His father had already disappeared.

Since his birth, John had always taken for granted the love of his grandma Perkins and of his aunts and uncles. It was always there. Now he had another love to cling to — even if it was just a memory — the love of a father.

That night John cried himself to sleep in the cornshuck bed. For a brief time, he had had a daddy. And he had lost him.

3

Bootleggers

Rosie Lee!" John hissed. "Hide! Here comes the sheriff!"

John pointed toward the road. The police cruiser had stopped at the roadside, and from it, two large white men emerged.

The two Perkins cousins were prepared. They dove into a clump of bushes and looked out through the leaves, watching as the sheriff and his deputy approached.

"Got to be some moonshine in these parts somewhere," Sheriff Calbourn muttered, kicking at the ground.

The deputy swung his billy club at some bushes. "I know that Coot woman sells the stuff," he said. "Everybody says so. But where does she hide it?"

John stifled a giggle. His aunt Coot was an expert in the bootlegging business. Mississippi was a "dry" state. According to its laws, alcoholic beverages could not be sold legally. These laws had encouraged a new business — the making and selling of moonshine.

Uncle Tom hauled the whiskey from stills hidden in the swamplands of Mississippi. Aunt Coot and other members of the Perkins family kept enough moonshine in the house to sell each day and hid the rest in the woods behind the house.

John had helped to hide some of the whiskey. He and his cousins dug deep, narrow holes in which several jars could be stacked. To make the hideouts foolproof, they covered each hole with pine needles and a rotten pine stump.

John knew that one of those hideouts was nearby. From his hiding place in the bushes, he watched nervously as the sheriff and his deputy searched the woods for illegal moonshine.

John whispered to Rosie Lee, "Think they'll find it?"

"Nah," Rosie Lee said. "It's hidden too well."

"Shhhh," John placed his finger to his lips and edged deeper into the leaves and bushes. Rosie Lee followed her cousin's example. Neither of them wanted to get caught and have to answer questions from the sheriff.

Soon the two men walked within fifteen feet of the cousins' hiding place. With long sticks, they poked into the dirt and bushes, looking for glass jars.

"Maybe it's under this here stump," the sheriff said. Several months before, the sheriff had found some jars of moonshine under an old stump.

The men began to poke their sticks into the stump. But after several minutes of searching, they came up empty.

John and Rosie Lee hugged themselves with glee. They knew that some of their supplies were hidden under another stump only a few feet from where the men stood.

The men pulled out handkerchiefs and wiped their faces. "Wish we could find that stuff," the sheriff said. "It's got to be here somewhere."

John smothered a giggle with his hands. Although they didn't know it, the officers were standing exactly over another stash of whiskey.

Finally the men left, disgusted with their failure to find anything. As their car drove off down the road, John and his cousin tumbled out of the woods, laughing.

"Those dumb policemen," John crowed. "They couldn't find the noses on their faces if they tried."

4

No More School

"Tupey, you're going to school today," Grandma called.

His room was still pitch black, but John leaped out of bed and pulled on some clothes. *School*, John thought. *School is what my cousins have been talking about for years, and now I finally get to see it. Guess that's where I learn my letters and numbers.*

John hunched over his metal bowl and ate his breakfast as Aunt Ethel wrapped biscuits and jam in brown paper for his lunch.

"Hurry up now, or you'll be late for school," she told the cousins, handing them their lunches.

The Perkins cousins had a long walk ahead of them. The three-room schoolhouse was five miles away. It held eight grades and was run by three teachers. For a rural school, Greenwood Elementary was large, enrolling about ninety students.

To break up their long walk, the Perkins cousins sometimes stopped to throw rocks into a pond. All of the leaves on the large oak trees had fallen for the winter. The cotton fields were picked clean, and occasionally the children passed a small farmhouse near the road. When John felt the cool December wind, he dug his hands a little deeper into his pockets and pulled his cap a little tighter on his head.

Seeing a stone wall, John sat down to rest for a few minutes. The morning sunlight was beginning to peek over the horizon.

"John, we've got to keep walking or we'll be late," Rosie Lee said.

"It's a long way to school," John complained.

"Let's go, John," Rosie Lee encouraged. "I'd hate to see you get some licks on the first day for being late."

Reluctantly, John left his perch and trudged down the road alongside his cousin.

Soon they came to the paved highway that would take them into town. In the distance, John spotted a yellow school bus roaring toward them.

"Watch out!" Rosie Lee called, pulling John to the side of the road.

What's going on? John wondered as the bus drew near.

Then he saw them. The sneering, hateful white faces. "Move off the road, nigger!" a boy yelled.

Suddenly, a sharp pain stung John's arm. "Ow!" he cried as the bus roared past.

"They get you?" Rosie Lee asked.

John nodded, holding his arm. A large rock had left a bruise just over his elbow.

"Better watch out next time," Rosie Lee said. "They like to throw rocks and things at colored people."

John stared after the yellow bus, which was now just a dot on the horizon. White children went to a separate school. They had a school bus and didn't have to walk for miles to school like the black children. So why did they have to pick on him?

For the rest of the walk to school, John's heart was heavy. He hoped the rest of the day would be better.

As the cousins rounded a bend in the road, they could see the white wooden schoolhouse. *Ding! Ding!* A bell rang, calling them into school.

"Hurry up, Tupey!" Rosie Lee cried, breaking into a run.

John arrived at school out of breath. He followed his cousin into a room filled with younger students. Five rows of wooden desks filled the room. A big, black cast iron heater stood in the middle. Because of the cold, all the seats around the heater were already full.

"John Perkins," Miss Turner called to her new student. "Take this note home to your parents." John stuck the piece of paper into his pocket.

At home later that afternoon, Grandma Perkins read the note. "It says here that you need a book. Your aunt Ethel can take you into town."

Together, John and Aunt Ethel walked into New Hebron. In the drugstore, she pulled out twenty cents and purchased a small book for John. Now he could learn to read!

School lessons usually covered the three R's: reading, writing, and arithmetic. But one day, John's teacher lectured the class on how to brush their teeth properly.

"It's important to brush your teeth each day with a toothbrush," the teacher said. "And you need to make sure you use the right up-and-down strokes." The teacher drew some teeth on the blackboard and demonstrated.

On the way home, John turned to Rosie Lee. "What did you think about what the teacher said?"

"Would have helped if any of us had toothbrushes," Rosie Lee said with a smile.

"Yeah, I don't know a single person in the class who owns a toothbrush," John said. "It makes you wonder why we bother coming to school."

But John always had one good reason for coming to school — recess! At recess, John and his friends made little carts with wheels from sweet gum logs. Whenever they could get outside the classroom, they climbed on these carts and flew down the steep ravine behind the school. Occasionally, someone would get bruised, but an injury only added to the excitement.

*   *   *

One day in early March, Uncle Bud said, "It's time to start workin' in the fields. School's out for ya'll."

"Yea!" John and Rosie Lee cheered. The Perkins family had never put a high value on school and education. As sharecroppers, they lived from one crop to the next. Nothing — not even school — could interfere with their farming.

Everyone in the family, including the children, worked until the crops were harvested from the fields. Usually that work didn't end until late November or early December. Then the sharecroppers had a few months off until the cycle began again in early February, when they started clearing the land for the next crop.

So, the children of sharecroppers attended school for just three or four months a year instead of the usual eight. Instead of taking a year to finish first grade, students like John took two or three years because of their shortened school year.

For the first three years, John went to school about four months out of the year. Then for the next four years, he attended school only about three months a year. Before he reached the fourth grade, John was doing a man's work in the fields. And with the outbreak of World War II, he was needed there full-time.

John dropped out of school and never returned.

5

Tail Kicking

Boy, did TJ ever get his tail kicked last Saturday!" John said.

"Yeah," Jimmy sighed. "He sure was in the wrong place at the wrong time."

Tail kicking was common practice in Mississippi. White men would look for a black man to pick on, and when they found someone, they would kick him on his bottom. It was terribly humiliating. The victim had no choice but to run away, the roar of laughter in his ears. Fighting back would only bring harsher beating.

Saturday afternoon was a prime time for tail kicking. Work was finished for the week, and large crowds gathered on the streets of New Hebron.

One Saturday, John asked Clyde if he could go to town with him.

"Sure, Tupey," Clyde said. Twelve years older than John, Clyde was like a father to him.

The two Perkins boys headed into town. Soon they were walking down the main street, where brick buildings lined the road and people stood in small groups, gossiping and laughing.

The brothers were about to join a group of their friends when a big white man approached them. It was DeWitt Armstrong. Clyde tried to move out of his path.

"Hey, nigger," DeWitt taunted Clyde. "What you doing here in town, huh?"

Clyde walked on, stone-faced. John almost ran to keep up with his long strides. His heart beat fiercely.

"I'm talkin' to you, nigger," the man continued taunting Clyde. "You listen to me."

The man came closer. John's heart was in his throat. Clyde was big and strong, but if he struck DeWitt, the white men would surely beat him to get even.

Then, out of the corner of his eye, John saw it happen. DeWitt lifted his foot and kicked Clyde on his backside.

Clyde stumbled and fell into the dirt. Giggles and hoots rang through the streets.

John backed away. *Oh, oh*, he thought. *Watch out, DeWitt*. He knew that Clyde didn't take guff from anyone. Not even from a white man.

Slowly, Clyde picked himself up and dusted off his pants. Then he turned and faced his tormentor.

In one quick motion, Clyde doubled his fist and swung. One punch was all it took. DeWitt fell flat into the street.

Several white men rushed to DeWitt's side. "DeWitt," one called. "Are you okay? Say something."

DeWitt didn't move. Clyde had knocked him unconscious.

The laughter of a few minutes before was quickly replaced with silence and stares.

"Come on, John. Let's get out of here," Clyde said. Without another word, the two brothers strode out of town.

The whites in New Hebron didn't know what to do next. Usually such rebellion from a black person created a mob scene. The whites instantly banded together and took out their hatred on the black person with a beating. Sometimes they even killed blacks who rebelled.

But Clyde was different. Everyone knew that Clyde was a Perkins and that two of his uncles, Bill and Bud, were rough characters. As bootleggers, they considered themselves above the law and wouldn't hesitate to take revenge.

DeWitt began to stir. He rubbed his eyes and shook his head to clear it. Grumbling, he climbed slowly to his feet.

"Let's get that Perkins," he growled.

"Best leave well enough alone, DeWitt," one of his friends advised.

DeWitt burned with anger. He would never forget that punch.

*   *   *

Clyde's "uppity" attitude apparently was not forgotten in New Hebron. Several years later, young men were being drafted to fight in World War II. The draft boards were made up of white men, who decided which young men would go to war.

Clyde was one of the first to receive his draft notice. In a few weeks, he reported for duty and soon was sent overseas.

6

Cheated!

The rows of cotton stretched out in front of nine-year-old John Perkins. All day long, John had been rapidly stuffing the fluffy white balls into his sack.

Will I ever be able to pick 200 pounds of cotton in a day? he wondered. Two hundred pounds was the daily goal for each man. For reaching that goal, a man earned a dollar. Despite his hard work, John had never come close.

At noon, John hauled his sack of cotton to be weighed.

"Forty-eight pounds," Mr. Bush droned, recording the number. A look of surprise flashed across

33

John's face. If he continued working at the same rate, he might be able to pick 100 pounds!

Like John, every child constantly tried to increase the amount of cotton he could pick. As the pounds increased, each child edged closer to manhood.

John ate his lunch quickly and hurried back to his row in the cotton fields. He leaned over and picked as fast as he could. *Today, I'm going for 100 pounds*, he thought.

At the end of the day, John stood in line to have his sack weighed once more by Fred Bush, the plantation owner. "Forty-two pounds of cotton," Mr. Bush said, eyeing the scale. He added John's numbers from the morning and the afternoon. Then the old man gave John a long look.

"That's almost 100 pounds, John. Good work." Mr. Bush turned to the next person in line, but his words echoed in John's ears. Such encouragement from the owner was rare. At nine years old, John had worked like a man.

John walked a little taller on the way home, jingling his ninety cents in his pocket. Now he had a new standard for work — he had to pick at least ninety pounds every day.

Over the next three years, John grew rapidly. He became known as a hard, fast worker. Before long, he was consistently picking over 100 pounds of cotton and earning over a dollar a day.

One summer, twelve-year-old John lived away from home with a friend. Mr. Lee, a white man from a plantation nearby, was hauling hay.

"I need someone to help," Mr. Lee told the young Perkins. "It's looking like rain, and unless I do something in a hurry, it will ruin my hay."

John thought for a few minutes. *I could use a day of work*, he thought. *I could earn myself at least $1.50.*

"Sure, I'll work for you today," John agreed. He began immediately, trusting Mr. Lee to pay him the usual rate.

Throughout the day, John and Mr. Lee threw bales of hay onto a wagon. They worked fast, as dark clouds threatened.

The hay scratched as it rubbed against John's arms, but he worked hard, keeping pace with Mr. Lee.

Finally, the hay was hauled out of the field and into the barn. The work was finished.

"John, good work," Mr. Lee said. "Here's your wages." Reaching inside his pocket, he pulled out a dime and a buffalo nickel.

Fifteen cents for sweating all day in the field! John had made more money picking cotton back home!

John didn't know what to do. If he rejected the money or complained, the white farmer would accuse him of being an "uppity nigger." John knew that a black person considered a "smart mouth" would have a hard time getting any other work in Mississippi. He recognized that he was being cheated and used like a slave, but he was afraid to complain. Extending his hand, John took the dime and nickel from Mr. Lee.

As John walked down the road toward home, he thought about his day's work. This white man had taken advantage of him. But Mr. Lee had several advantages over John. He owned land and hay, the basic materials to make money. And he owned a wagon and horses to haul his hay into the barn.

And what do I own? John wondered. *Just my hands and strong back for work.* Because he didn't have any possessions, John felt helpless.

If I'm going to make it in this world, I've got to have either the basic materials or the means to make those materials, John thought. *If you have those materials, then you can use them for good or for evil. Mr. Lee used them against me for evil.*

Deep inside, John boiled with rage.

7

Bargaining

In December of 1943, twelve-year-old John and his cousin Jimmy contracted to cut pulp wood for a local businessman. The two boys borrowed a crosscut saw and went to work right away.

As John and Jimmy sawed, they talked and dreamed about how they would spend their hard-earned money. "It sure will be great to get $5 for each load," Jimmy remarked. What are you going to do with your money?"

For an instant, John stopped moving the saw back and forth.

"I'm needing a new shirt," he said. "I'll probably use the money for that."

After several days of hard work, the pair calculated that they had earned about $9 each, a total of $18 for several loads of wood.

Eagerly, they went to their boss for payment. To their surprise, the lanky man reached into his wallet and pulled out a $10 bill instead of the full $18.

The white man knew the correct wage but figured he wouldn't get any complaints from the boys. Cheating black people was an everyday occurrence in his part of the country.

"Hey, we're supposed to get more money for that truckload," John told the man.

His mouth dropped open, and his face turned red with anger. "Who do you think you are, talking to me like that?" he yelled.

The boys stood silently, staring him down.

"What are you going to do about it?" Mr. Harrington finally asked.

"We're going to quit," John said firmly. "We're not going to cut any more of your wood."

Suddenly, Mr. Harrington was speechless. They had him cornered, and they knew it.

Without another word, the boys turned on their heels and left.

During this time, the Perkins family lived about five miles from town. Every Wednesday evening, most of their community headed into town to see a movie. The Perkins family also went. Mr. Harrington lived about seven miles from town and had to drive his wood truck past the Perkins home. Usually, he stopped to pick up moviegoers.

The next Wednesday evening on their way to the movies, John and Jimmy heard the roar of Mr. Harrington's wood truck.

"There it is, Jimmy," John said, gesturing toward the green pickup. "Our ride to town."

The two boys waved their hands to stop Mr. Harrington. When he didn't slow down at all, they grabbed onto the back of the moving truck and swung on. They plopped down beside others in the back and made it into town.

Later that evening, John and Jimmy again tried to jump onto the back of Mr. Harrington's truck to catch a ride home. But, this time, they missed. In a huge cloud of dust, Mr. Harrington roared past the Perkins boys.

"What's with him?" Jimmy asked John. "We always ride with him."

"He's paying us back because we didn't cut his wood," John said. It was unusual for blacks to challenge pay rates or accuse their white employers of cheating. Mr. Harrington turned against John and Jimmy because they had questioned his unjust business practices.

At this time, the Perkins family lived on a plantation owned by Cliff Mobley. John and Jimmy were the youngest boys in the Perkins family. The older boys had joined the army and were fighting in World War

II. It was up to John and Jimmy to care for their elderly grandmother.

When the seasons changed from summer to fall, the Perkins family shifted crops. By the middle of October, they had finished picking the cotton crop and shifted to corn. Once all the corn had been pulled at the end of October, the sugar cane crop had to be harvested.

In early November, John and Jimmy headed into the sugar cane fields. Using sharp knives, they stripped off the leaves, then clipped the top and cut the cane. Finally, they stacked it on the edge of the field.

For a day's work of cutting sugar cane, John and Jimmy each got a gallon of syrup. They could sell the syrup for $1.50 or keep it for their morning biscuits.

As day laborers, the boys always enjoyed a noon meal with the Mobley family. In the kitchen dining room, everyone sat around the table and heaped their plates with potatoes, green vegetables, and meat.

The culture in Mississippi demanded that whites and blacks be separated. But Cliff Mobley and many other country farmers saw no need to separate their laborers from themselves. Everyone had to eat.

But one day when John and Jimmy came in for lunch, they noticed a dramatic change. Mrs. Mobley's mother, Mrs. Wilson, had arrived to help with the cooking because her daughter was pregnant.

Mrs. Wilson, who was from a more traditional southern family, refused to let the boys sit with the rest of her family. Instead, John and Jimmy had to sit at a small kitchen table and eat after the Mobleys had finished.

John and Jimmy couldn't believe the poor quality and small quantity of food they received. *You cooked this for our lunch?* they thought. *Forget it.* The boys walked off the job and returned home.

An hour later, Mr. Mobley showed up at their door, his face red with anger. "What's the problem here?" he said. "Why aren't you boys working?"

"We didn't get enough food," John said calmly.

"Yeah, and what we got wasn't any good," Jimmy added.

Mr. Mobley took off his hat and scratched the top of his head. After thinking for a few minutes, he asked, "If my parents fed you lunch, would you go back to work?"

"It's a deal, Mr. Mobley," the boys said. That afternoon, they returned to work in the cane fields.

In that exchange, John and Jimmy had learned the power of collective bargaining. The two cousins recognized their value as workers. They knew they did good work. And when they banded together, they were strong enough to protect themselves from being cheated for that work. Even without owning property, they could bargain for better pay and other benefits.

8

The Shooting

When Clyde Perkins was serving in the United States Army overseas, the Perkinses didn't hear much news from him. One day, though, they learned that Clyde had been wounded several times in Germany. For those injuries, Clyde received several combat ribbons, a Purple Heart medal, and, finally, an honorable discharge from the service. Clyde headed home to New Hebron, Mississippi.

Eager to see Clyde again, John and the rest of the family gathered at the bus stop. Sixteen-year-old John was the first to spot the long gray bus.

"There he is!" he cried.

The family cheered as the bus pulled to a stop. Soon, there was Clyde himself, climbing down the step with his duffel bag slung over his shoulder. He stood tall in his military uniform, decorated with a row of ribbons. Through his military service, Clyde had gained self-respect.

"Here, Clyde, let me carry that," John said, reaching for the duffel bag.

"You have to tell us all about it," Jimmy said excitedly. "We want to hear everything."

But Clyde wasn't listening. He was looking around, checking out the town.

"Everything looks exactly as I remembered it," he remarked.

"Pretty much," Jimmy said. "Only now DeWitt Armstrong's the mayor. You'd better watch out for him, Clyde. He still hasn't forgiven you for punching him out that time."

Clyde laughed. "Huh. DeWitt doesn't scare me. I've seen worse."

John warned him, "Yeah, but he and the marshal have burrs in their behinds against black folks."

"Who's the marshal now?" Clyde asked.

"Bud Thurman," John replied. "We know for a fact he's killed some black men around here."

Clyde's face tightened. And John noticed.

He's come back from one war, he thought. *And now he's got to fight another.*

On a Saturday evening a few weeks later, John and Clyde walked to town together. Clyde was going to take his girlfriend to the movies, and John was going to visit some friends.

Stopping in front of Riley's General Merchandise to talk with some friends, they spotted a disturbance down the street.

It was Marshal Thurman. He was swaggering through the crowds, swinging his billy club. A young black man didn't see him approach, and the marshal growled at him.

"Get off the streets, nigger." His voice echoed down the suddenly quiet street. And he swung his club, hitting the young man in the ribs.

The young man backed away, saying nothing, and Thurman swaggered on.

"Did you see that?" Clyde said in a low voice.

"Uh-huh," John said.

The two brothers watched, burning with anger.

"There's no reason to treat folks like that," Clyde muttered.

The sun slipped behind the main buildings. It was getting late, and blacks were expected to be off the streets by 8:30 P.M.

"I'm heading over to Charlie's," John said. "Say hi to Elma for me."

"Sure," Clyde agreed. He turned and headed for the alley near Carolyn's Theater, where he planned to meet his girlfriend, Elma.

The theater had two entrances. Whites used the

big, glass double doors in front. Blacks used a side entrance and climbed the stairs to the theater balcony.

The alley leading to the side door was crowded with people waiting for the ticket booth to open. People grew tired of waiting and began to push and shove.

"What's going on, Clyde?" Elma asked.

"I don't know. Let's stay out of it," Clyde said.

The couple stepped back to the edge of the crowd, away from the pushing.

The noise and tension grew. Everyone was aware when the marshal and his deputy appeared in the crowd.

"You niggers quiet down," the marshal yelled.

Clyde had his back to the marshal, but the man pulled out his nightstick and clubbed him in the shoulder. Clyde spun around, but seeing that Thurman was going to hit him a second time, he grabbed Thurman's arm to stop his swing.

Thurman's eyes flashed with anger. Stepping back two steps, he pulled out his gun and shot Clyde twice in the stomach.

As soon as the shots rang out, silence fell over the crowd. The marshal and his deputy turned and walked away as a crowd of blacks surrounded Clyde. Several men gently picked up Clyde and carried him across the street to Seay's Drugstore. The back of the store was a doctor's office.

John was still at his friend's house about a half a mile away when word came that Clyde had been shot.

John jumped into a car and arrived at the drugstore a few minutes later.

Without knowing any details, John was certain a white man had shot his brother. Anger stirred deep inside him. *I want to get even,* he thought. *What will it take?*

At the drugstore, John found a crowd of people already in the doctor's office. Pushing his way inside, John saw Clyde on the examining table. John overheard the news: "The marshal shot him."

The only white faces in the room were Thurman, his deputy, Doctor Langston, and another officer. The angry voices in the room mixed with the crowd that had gathered outside the windows. Tension mounted.

As the black faces watched the doctor work, Marshal Thurman stood by and watched the room. While more people jammed into the small office, John moved closer to his brother. He watched as the doctor frantically worked on Clyde's wounds. Putting his hand on his brother's cheek, John begged Clyde, "Don't die."

Doctor Langston looked up. "You'll have to get him to a hospital. I can't do anything else for him here."

The crowd began to buzz. "Somebody get a car so Clyde can get to the hospital!"

Soon John's cousin Joe David pulled his 1941 Chevy to the back door. Clyde was carefully lifted onto the backseat. John and his uncle Bill climbed in beside him. Two others scrambled into the front with Joe, and the car peeled off toward Jackson, the state capital and site of the nearest hospital. The trip would take at least an hour and a half.

As John held Clyde's head, his brother tossed and turned with pain. "Clyde, you've got to live," John pleaded. "You can't die."

The car sped past large homes and small sharecropper shacks, past cotton fields and tall pine trees. Finally, it entered the Jackson city limits and reached the hospital. Other cars from New Hebron also arrived. Everyone waited and waited.

At one point during the night, John entered the treatment room to see his brother for a few minutes. Clyde lay there with a blood pressure cuff strap around his arm. He didn't speak, but John spoke softly to him.

Much later, a man came to the waiting room with an announcement. Clyde was dead.

John burned with anger. Clyde had fought for the United States in another country. But he had been gunned down in his own hometown by a fellow American.

John's rage soon turned to numbness. In a daze, he left the hospital and sat through Clyde's funeral and burial service.

At the cemetery of the Oak Ridge Baptist Church, an undertaker, not a pastor, spoke about Clyde. The Perkinses weren't churchgoers. John stared into space as the man spoke. The blue coffin lay open, but the person inside didn't look like John's brother.

Finally, attendants closed the coffin and lowered

it into the grave. As the grave was sealed, the matter was closed for the people in New Hebron.

Investigating the shooting would be pointless. Everyone knew who held the power: the whites.

* * *

"What are we going to do now?" Uncle Bud asked a few days later during a family meal. The Perkins family had a reputation for toughness. Neighbors knew not to argue with a member of the Perkins family — especially Uncle Bud or Uncle Bill.

"We'd better lie low," suggested Uncle Bill calmly. "It would be a good idea if some of us left the area for a while."

Uncle Bud agreed. "We've got to get John out of Mississippi," he said. The family agreed. A few days later, some of the family left for California. John moved to Jackson and lived with his aunt Lillie Mae, who ran a boarding house for blacks.

But Jackson was still too close to New Hebron. The family was worried about John's safety. So, after several months, Aunt Lillie Mae and Uncle Bud earned enough money to send John out west.

Fearing for his life, John packed a lunch and one change of clothes in a small bag. He boarded a train to California with just $3 in his pocket and watched the plains of Texas flow into New Mexico, Arizona, and then California.

I've gotten out of Mississippi, John told himself. *Forever!*

9

Strike!

California. Land of opportunity. John knew immediately that this place was different.

Over the years, many of John's relatives had fled Mississippi to move to California. During World War II when a black man was beaten to death, two cousins, Willa Mae Perkins and Tommy Perkins, had moved to California. When John arrived, he moved in with Tommy and ate his meals with Willa Mae.

Many of the Mississippi blacks had settled into the northern Los Angeles suburb of Monrovia. The gentle palm trees swayed in the breezes from the nearby ocean. John loved the low humidity, mild temperatures, and warm sunshine.

Almost immediately, John found a job in the Union Pacific Foundry. He couldn't believe how much he earned — ninety-eight cents an hour. In 1947, that was a lot of money. In Mississippi, John had earned just $20 a month for backbreaking work.

But good weather and money weren't the only reasons John loved California.

Growing up in the South, John's every action had been restricted by his color. It determined where he could work and where he could socialize. It meant separation from whites at school, at stores, even at public drinking fountains.

But in California, John worked alongside whites and received the same wages. The Union Pacific Foundry had opened in the flurry of economic activity that followed World War II. Workers of all colors were desperately needed and equally respected. Along with two white men, John joined the crew that cast iron pipes for sewage and plumbing.

In the first six months, several members of the crew quit, but John stayed. Soon John knew more about casting work than anyone else on the crew.

Management was pleased with the progress in the factory. Production increased dramatically, and the company earned lots of money. But one thing gave them trouble — the union. The workers had banded together to change their working conditions.

One day after work, John attended a union meeting.

"We deserve better," the union leader said. "After all, we're the ones who turned around the production, and we should share in the extra profits. If not, then we should strike."

"I agree," John said. "In Mississippi, I learned the power of our labor. It's what we can bargain with to make changes around here."

When the workers approached the company, however, its managers said, "We're not in a position to raise your pay. We can't help you."

"Then you've given us no other choice," the union leader said. "We're going on strike and setting up picket lines in front of the factory."

So John and the other union officials stopped working. Because of their united efforts, the factory production came to a screeching halt. The company officials stood firm for several days but quickly realized their defeat.

"Bob, this isn't going to change," the company manager said to the owner. "We'd better do something to raise their pay."

The company announced an increase that would be tied to production. As the workers produced more pipes, their pay would increase. It was the solution John had proposed at the union meeting several days before.

The workers cheered the news. The strike was

over, and they returned to work. Immediately, John enjoyed the results of their united efforts. His pay increased, and at times he earned $100 per week.

If we can work together, we can change the system, John thought. *It may not happen overnight, but there is power in working together for change.*

It was an unforgettable lesson.

10

Vera Mae

The August sunshine was bright as John stepped outside his family cabin in Mississippi. It was 1949, and John had returned from California for a brief visit.

"Junior, let's get over to that church revival this afternoon," John suggested to his cousin.

"Good idea," Junior agreed.

Church revivals were more than religious meetings. These huge gatherings were opportunities for people to socialize. People gathered from different churches around the county and set up booths to sell every kind of food. Five times more people came to the churchyard than could fit into the church.

When the boys arrived at the churchyard, it was already packed. Like many of the young people, John was there strictly to meet people. He had no interest in God or attending the service.

Inside, the church service was about to end. Soon the congregation poured out of the church and spilled out onto the lawn.

John noticed a tall, dark, good-looking girl at the top of the church steps. Instantly John knew why he had come to this particular meeting.

I've got to meet that girl, John thought, then tried to figure out how to begin a conversation.

Vera Mae Buckley walked down the church steps and over to her father's car with a girlfriend. The two of them sat in the car talking while John continued to watch. John thought, *This is the girl I'm going to marry.*

"What a nice-looking car!" John said to strike up a conversation with the girls. They introduced themselves and told him where they lived. John said he had just arrived from California.

The Buckley family was one of the few black families who owned a small farm. As churchgoers, the Buckleys had always been a little suspicious of the bootlegging, unchurched Perkins family. Despite these reservations, Vera Mae continued talking with John in front of the church.

After a few minutes John said, "I know who would make me a good wife. I'm sort of looking for a wife."

Although John had changed the subject suddenly, Vera Mae didn't laugh.

Instead she smiled and asked, "You do? Who?"

"Vera Mae," John said. "You're going to be my wife someday."

Vera Mae was startled by the sudden marriage proposal. She didn't instantly accept, but she didn't say no, either.

* * *

A few days later, John returned to California. For the next two years, John and Vera Mae didn't see each other, but they kept the post office busy with a chain of letters. After a few months, John knew that his first impression of Vera Mae had been correct. He wanted her as his wife.

One afternoon in the fall, John and his cousin Tommy sat on the back steps talking. It had been a long day at the factory, and they were resting. "We need to settle down and get married," John said out of the blue.

"That's a good idea, but who are you going to marry?" Tommy asked.

"All these California girls seem so shallow," John said. "Nobody's like Vera Mae Buckley."

"Then maybe you ought to marry her," Tommy suggested.

"If she will say yes," John said. Soon the conversation drifted off into other topics. But John day-dreamed about Vera Mae.

*   *   *

In 1950, a piece of paper put an end to nineteen-year-old John's dreams. It was a draft notice. The Korean War was in full swing, and John was needed in the army.

Before he reported for basic training at Fort Ord in Salinas, California, John took another trip to Mississippi. He wanted to see friends and family, but especially Vera Mae, who had finished high school and was teaching at a little country school.

John spent every spare moment with Vera Mae, certain that he wanted to marry her. But every time John talked about marriage, Vera Mae quickly changed the subject. She never answered his proposal, so John returned to California alone.

As soon as John got back to Monrovia, he went straight to Fort Ord for his basic training. After fifteen weeks of basic training, John still Couldn't get Vera Mae out of his mind. As soon as he got out on furlough, he picked up the telephone and called Mississippi.

"Vera Mae, can you come to California to marry me?" he asked.

There was a long pause. Then Vera Mae said, "I've got to ask my momma." After another long silence,

Vera Mae returned to the phone. "Yes. I can come to California."

Eighteen-year-old Vera Mae had a train to catch!

* * *

Three days later, John, Vera Mae, and three friends drove to Yuma, Arizona for the marriage ceremony. The state of California required blood tests for a marriage and then a waiting period of several days. John and Vera Mae wanted to be married as soon as possible before John went overseas. A wedding in Arizona would be faster.

The trip took the entire morning, and they arrived in the early afternoon. John and Vera Mae found a wedding chapel for blacks.

"Where do we get our license?" John asked the owner. They signed the wedding license with their friends as the witnesses; then the short service began. John and Vera Mae were filled with excitement. They were becoming husband and wife!

"That will be $10 please," the owner said after he finished the service.

John was floored. He had been so excited about the service that he had forgotten to ask about the price.

John pulled out a ten dollar bill and handed it to the man. To this owner, weddings were strictly business. But to John, this wedding marked the beginning of the most special relationship in his life.

11

The Ladder of Success

John and Vera Mae returned to Monrovia, but their time together was brief. Twenty-one days later, John traveled to the island group called Okinawa for eighteen lonely months. While John was gone, Vera Mae returned to Mississippi. Once again, they wrote many letters to stay in touch.

January of 1953 marked a new year and new opportunities for John. After his discharge from the army, he went straight to his cousin's house in Monrovia, California. *I've got to get back to Vera Mae,* John thought. He planned to go immediately to Mississippi. While there, John could also see his father again.

Throughout his life, John had tried to stay in touch with his father. John knew his dad loved him, but they didn't see each other very often. While John was overseas, Jap Perkins had suffered a heart attack. Since his illness, Jap had been staying with Aunt Coot in New Hebron. Aunt Coot had been the center of John's Mississippi family. Through letters from her, John had stayed up-to-date about various members of his family.

But instead of John going to Mississippi, Vera Mae came to California and brought news about his father. "Your dad is getting better, John," Vera Mae told him. "He seems to be out of danger."

"That's a relief," John said. "Now I don't need to return to Mississippi to see Daddy right away." Together, he and Vera Mae could forge a new life in California.

A few weeks later, John received a telephone call. "Jap died last night," Aunt Coot told him. "You'd better come home."

The next day, John flew back to New Hebron to bury his father. After the funeral, relatives and friends crowded into the house and told stories about John's father.

"He hoped you'd come home right after you got out of the service, Tupey," Aunt Coot said as she dabbed the corner of her eye with a white handkerchief. "At that time, Jap'd only been sick for about a week and was getting better. He'd been wishing that you'd come for a visit."

John listened with a mixture of sadness and wonder. Ever since his father disappeared from his life, John had questioned whether his father wanted him. And now he learned that Jap had!

After a long pause, John asked, "Why, Aunt Coot? Why didn't you let me know that my father wanted me to come home?"

Aunt Coot fell into deep thought. She was trying to find the right words. "Jap knew that Vera Mae was here in New Hebron. He thought it'd be natural for you to come and get her. So he didn't make any special requests. But when you didn't come get her, he felt really bad because he knew you weren't coming."

John listened sadly, sorry now that he had missed his last chance to see his father alive.

On the way home, John thought about his scattered family. And he thought about those he would never see again. Mother. Daddy. Clyde.

But as the train rolled on, John began to push his sad thoughts aside. More than ever, he was determined to return to California and pursue the good life. In that land of sunshine, he could forget all of the bitterness of his past and press on to a new life and new dreams.

Back in California, John looked for a new job. He didn't want something easy. He wanted something with opportunity. Finally, he took a job as a janitor with the Shopping Bag Food Store Company.

After a couple of years, John talked with the company president. "I'd like to stay with the company, but I need to move up," John explained.

"We've got a new position in our welding shop," the president said. "But you'd have to go through some training."

"I'm ready for it," John told him.

Within a week, John had a new job.

John quickly showed his supervisor that he could learn any new machinery. Soon he discovered that he could easily build shopping carts or bakery bins — whatever equipment was needed. He could even organize and supervise others. John began to climb the ladder of success within the company. Slowly, his dreams were becoming reality.

12

Sunday School

While John's work was getting exciting, his family was falling apart. John knew that his marriage was in trouble. He had no idea how to treat a woman properly.

One day Vera Mae told him, "I'm leaving, Tupey. I'm packing my bags and moving back to Mississippi." John let her go.

Vera Mae was two months pregnant with their first child when John and Vera Mae separated. Eight months after Spencer was born, they reunited. Their separation had given them time to think about their family and the importance of their relationship. They moved into their own home in California and began to make some new friends. At last, both John's work and family life seemed secure. But success at work and family didn't seem to be enough. John still didn't feel joy or peace.

John began wondering about things beyond work and family. *There are some big questions in life that I've never answered*, he thought. *Like, is there a God?*

In the spring of 1957, Spencer began attending a children's Bible class at a little church down the street from the Perkins's home.

"Spencer's awfully happy these days," John commented to Vera Mae.

"It's his Bible class at the church," she said. "He's learning so much there."

The Perkins family had never said a blessing or prayer before meals. But, having learned Bible verses in his classes, Spencer began reciting them before the family ate. The first verse was, "Jesus said, 'Follow me and I will make you fishers of men.' "

Sounds strange, John thought. *How do you fish for men?* The idea was completely new, but he was glad that the Bible class gave Spencer such joy. As Spencer shared more and more songs and Bible verses, John began to see the world through the eyes of his young son. "Jesus died for me, Daddy!" he told John.

But, unlike Spencer who celebrated Jesus in his life, John experienced only God's judgment. *God is going to send me to hell*, John thought. *I don't know what to do to trust God.*

"Daddy, will you come with me to Sunday school

and church?" Spencer asked one day. Because of his deep love for Spencer, John agreed to go.

In church, the preacher taught a lesson about God's love. Throughout his life, John had felt uncertain about love. For the first time, John heard a new idea about God — that God loved John Perkins.

"God loves you enough to send his Son to die on the cross for your sins," the preacher said. John thought, *I still remember that embrace as a small child from my father. It cost God a great deal to send his Son to die for me.*

A few days later, Mrs. Willie Price, a friend of Vera Mae's, invited John to attend a Tuesday night Bible study in a storefront building in El Monte, California. At his first meeting, John immediately noticed that he was the only black man in the room. He had never been in a church with white and black people together. John wondered if he would be turned away. But he had such a strong desire to study the Bible that he walked to the back of the room, determined to stay. By the end of the lesson, John knew why he had attended the study. Wayne Leitch, the teacher, had a deep love of the Scriptures and a willingness to teach others.

As the other people left the room, John hung back to shake hands with Mr. Leitch. But when John reached out to the teacher, Mr. Leitch didn't shake his hand. Instead, the gentle teacher wrapped his arm around John's shoulders. John could feel the love of God from this man. He promised himself that he would return and continue studying the Bible with Mr. Leitch.

The next Sunday morning, John went with a friend to Bethlehem Church of Christ Holiness. Vera Mae stayed home because she was pregnant and not feeling well. As John followed the pastor's sermon in his Bible, he couldn't believe what he was hearing. The pastor read from the sixth chapter of Romans: "For the wages of sin is death, but the gift of God is eternal life in Christ Jesus our Lord."

John knew about earning wages. For John, money was a symbol of a man's value. As a boy in Mississippi, John had worked a hard day and earned only fifteen cents. Before leaving the state, John had a job that made $20 a month. Now in California, he earned over $60 a week. In John's eyes, his worth had increased.

Yet how can wages be paid for a man? John wondered. *Especially a bootlegging Perkins?* Then John understood. Without God, death was the only payment for his sin, but God created a new way. John's debt had been paid through the death of Jesus Christ. The realization was like turning on a light switch in a completely dark room. John made a decision to follow Christ with his life.

For the rest of the sermon, John could hardly wait for the invitation. John wanted to make a public promise to follow Christ. He walked proudly to the front of the church to give his life to Jesus.

13

Prison Camp

I love to tell the story" begins an old hymn. John Perkins modeled that song. Overwhelmed by what Christ had done for his life, he began to tell anyone who would listen about how they too could discover joy.

A few days after John confessed his sins and put his faith in Christ for salvation, one of Vera Mae's friends, Wilnor Price, invited the Perkinses to attend Bible classes offered by Child Evangelism. The lessons were completely new to John. He loved learning new Bible stories and teaching them to others.

Every day at 4:00 P.M., John and Vera Mae gathered the children in their neighborhood and taught them about Jesus, using the Child Evangelism materials. Every Tuesday evening, they attended a training workshop for leaders. John took his decision to follow Jesus seriously — it was all or nothing.

The Tuesday Leaders Workshops gave the Perkinses opportunities to meet and talk with white Christians. For John it marked a new experience. "God's Word is a powerful force in our lives," Wayne Leitch, the teacher and Presbyterian elder, said. "When we struggle with the problems in our lives, we can draw strength and courage from the promises in the Bible." In a new way, John understood that God's love knew no racial barriers. Through Jesus Christ, God had touched mankind in a new and powerful way. Lives could be transformed through His grace.

Over the next three years, John studied the Bible with Wayne Leitch. John's assurance of his salvation increased. At the same time, John's drive for success and financial gain in the business world began to decrease. Instead of trusting in himself, John decided to put his business life into God's capable hands.

John continued to look for new opportunities to tell others about Jesus. One of them changed the direction of his life. One day a local bookstore owner asked, "John, how about joining our Christian Businessmen's Committee?" John agreed.

After getting acquainted with John, the men

asked John to share his testimony. John began to speak at several businessmen's lunches in the area.

After one of these lunches, two of John's friends, Ed Anthony and Dean Saum, stopped him. "John, we'd like you to go with us on Sunday to a prison camp in the San Bernardino Mountains." Boys between the ages of thirteen and seventeen filled this camp. Their work was cutting down trees in the mountains and preventing forest fires.

"Sure," John said, "I'd be glad to go with you."

At an old World War II-style hut, John and his two friends began a Sunday morning Bible class. Most of the thirty boys who sat in the hard metal chairs fidgeted and looked bored. They didn't care about what John was saying, but the meeting gave them something to do.

Despite the boys' attitude, John explained how God had worked in his life, and he told stories from the Bible. At the invitation, two of the boys came forward to confess their need for Christ.

On his way back to Monrovia, John thought about the meeting. He understood the young black prisoners because his background was similar to theirs. He had experienced their fears, their anger, and the obstacles that stood in their way. Like John, they had fled the lifestyle in the South and come to sunny California. Each of them had been filled with dreams, dreams that had been shattered.

As John thought about the young men in prison,

he felt a new sense of responsibility. *God wants me to return to Mississippi,* John thought. *That way I can help my people start new lives and build new dreams right where they are.*

A few weeks later, John spoke to Arcadia Union Church, an all-white church in Arcadia, California. John read the first verses of Romans 10: "Brothers, my heart's desire and prayer to God for the Israelites is that they might be saved. For I can testify about them that they are zealous for God, but their zeal is not based on knowledge."

That night, John heard God speak to him: "Return to Mississippi and teach your people."

Never again could John find satisfaction in his work in California. He needed to return to the land of his birth.

14

God's Will

You're going to do *what*!" Tommy Perkins exclaimed. He couldn't believe that John would even consider returning to Mississippi. "You've got it made here in California, John. Five-bedroom home. Good job. Great possibilities for other jobs. You'll throw away all that and return to Mississippi?"

Several of John's aunts and uncles also discouraged him from returning home. Over the years, John had helped a number of his relatives travel to California, find jobs, and settle into the area. Now all of a sudden, John was going to return to the South.

Learning of his plans, they looked at John as if he had lost his mind.

But John felt something the others didn't — a calling from God. He could never be at peace unless he obeyed God's will.

A few people understood John's decision to return. The members of his neighborhood Bible study group pledged monthly support and prayers. Two all-white churches in the area had a growing awareness of the need to help the black community, and they too had pledged support.

Vera Mae was stunned by John's plan to return to Mississippi. Her husband's decision to follow Christ made her happy, but not all his talk about going back home.

This "call of God" to return to Mississippi was John's call, not hers. The more John talked about it, the more vocal Vera Mae became about not wanting to leave.

*   *   *

One day, John couldn't spring out of bed with his usual energy. He walked a little slower to work. During the weeks that followed, John lost forty pounds, growing so weak that he could hardly stand. The doctors couldn't explain it.

Sometimes John talked about quitting his job at the food company, but Vera Mae said, "No, Tupey, you can't quit your job. You've got all these younguns to feed." Vera Mae was expecting their fifth child. So, even though he was sick, John continued struggling to work.

Then one day in November of 1959, John couldn't get out of bed. "I'll not be in to work today," John told his boss on the phone. "I'm sick and need to go to the doctor." It was very unusual for John to miss any work, but he didn't have the strength that day.

Doctors suspected liver trouble. But, after a battery of tests, the doctors couldn't find anything wrong. They prescribed vitamins to build up John's system. "Maybe he's just run down," they told Vera Mae. But, for the next several months, John continued to be sick. Over and over, Vera Mae took John to the Long Beach Veterans Hospital.

Vera Mae pretended that John's sickness didn't have anything to do with his "call" to return home. But inside she knew that John's decision and the sickness were connected.

Then Vera Mae received a clear message from God. If she didn't let John return to Mississippi, God would let her husband die. Vera Mae was terrified. That morning, she knelt by John's bed and prayed aloud: "Lord, it's a hard struggle for me to say yes, but I'm going to say yes. I'm not going to rebel any longer. I'm willing to go. I don't want to go, but I'm willing. Lord, I'm saying yes to you."

Then Vera Mae asked the Lord to touch John and give him strength. Suddenly, the heaviness on her heart lifted, and Vera Mae felt a new sense of peace. Soon after, John began to feel better and returned to work.

John continued to grow stronger. A few days before Thanksgiving, he told Vera Mae, "I'm going down to Mississippi to check things out." The next morning, he went with his family to the little bus station in Monrovia. As the bus pulled away from the station, the Perkins clan waved good-bye to John. All felt the loneliness of separation. No one knew what the future held.

John arrived in Mississippi on Thanksgiving Day. For several weeks, he spoke in local churches and talked with residents about his ideas for service. All the while, John thought of those black youths in the California prison camp. More than ever, he was convinced that his ministry would be among the young people in Mississippi. During the six weeks he was away from his family, John regained most of the weight he had lost during his unexplained illness, another sign to him that his life was headed in the right direction.

Just before Christmas, John rode the bus back to California. During the long ride home, John thought about Vera Mae. He knew that she was still hoping God would change his mind about Mississippi, and he appreciated Vera Mae's willingness to follow his lead.

When he reached California, John called Vera Mae. "Honey, it's me! Tupey! Can you come down and pick me up?"

"Sure, Tupey," Vera Mae said. "Where are you?"

"I'm right here in Monrovia," John said. "At the bus station. I just got back."

John could hear the joy in Vera Mae's voice. She was glad to have John home just in time for Christmas.

In January 1960, the Perkins's fifth child, Deborah, was born. John left his job and prepared to move his family to Mississippi. Vera Mae also quit her job in the beauty salon. During the next six months, the Perkins's financial needs were met by unexpected gifts from friends and churches. John continued speaking in churches throughout southern California and passing on his vision for a new ministry among his people in Mississippi.

By early June, all of their loose ends had been tied. John and Vera Mae loaded a trailer and hitched it to their '56 Chevy. The adventure of faith had begun. John's new ministry had the promise of $75 per month from two different churches. These funds would have to provide for two adults and five children.

The Perkinses headed south. Three days later, they were back in Mississippi. For good.

15

Polio

The small home of Vera Mae's grandmother in New Hebron changed overnight. On June 9, John and Vera and the five Perkins children — Spencer, Joanie, Phillip, Derek, and baby Deborah — arrived with their California belongings. The once-quiet house bustled with activity.

John hadn't lived in Mississippi for thirteen years, but little had changed there. Although the United States government had urged integration between blacks and whites, the white people of Mississippi had resisted such a drastic change in their way of life. Instead, they had promoted a policy of "separate but equal." Separate schools. Separate churches. Separate theater entrances.

John fit back into the community doing some manual labor such as chopping wood and picking cotton. At first some of his neighbors were embarrassed that John, now a preacher, had to do this type of work alongside them. He had traded a well-paying job, a comfortable home, and the freedom of California for a life of poverty and discomfort. But the work gave John the opportunity to renew old relationships. John rejoiced at the chance to share with others what Christ had done in his life.

John and Vera Mae immediately put into practice their training and experience from Child Evangelism. The black church was more accustomed to socializing than learning. The Perkinses started to turn this around. Throughout the rest of the summer, they organized vacation Bible schools in various churches, using flannel-graph pictures to teach Bible stories and bring them alive.

Each day, the Perkinses drove seven miles from New Hebron to Sophia Sutton's camp, where John taught Bible stories to a large class of children aged ten and up. There were 120 students, not including the mothers who listened intently from the back of the room. John and Vera's classes were so popular that requests poured in for John to set up additional vacation Bible schools and to speak in churches throughout the region. The Perkins's new life seemed to be off to a good start.

But one morning, Vera Mae announced some bad news. "John, Phillip's not getting any better." Several days earlier, the Perkinses had taken their four-year-old son to a local doctor. He was running a fever and beginning to limp, and the Perkins's crowded home without running water was a poor site for recovery. Phillip was growing worse.

"We need to take him to a specialist, but we can't afford it," John said. "What should we do?"

Vera Mae felt uneasy about Phillip. "Maybe we shouldn't have left California," she said. "You had a good job there, and we could afford to see the doctors. Going back might save Phillip's life."

John knew he was called to his work in Mississippi, but he worried about Phillip. Each morning, he got up early and went into a back room of the nearby church to pray. One morning as he prayed on his knees, John felt tremendous concern about his son. The choice seemed clear. Return to California for the necessary medical help or stay in Mississippi and bury his son.

As he opened his Bible, John's eyes fell on a section of Mark's gospel. "Lo we have left all and have followed thee," Peter tells Jesus. John identified with Peter. *Surely I have done the same,* John thought, eagerly reading Jesus' response: "Verily I say unto you, There is no man that has left house, or brethren, or sisters, or father, or mother, or wife, or children, or lands, for my sake and the gospels, But he shall receive an hundredfold now in this time . . . ; and in the world to come eternal life."

John then remembered Abraham, the great Old Testament figure who had been willing to sacrifice his only son, Isaac, if that was God's will. John made a decision. He would stay in Mississippi. As he finished his prayer, John felt certain that Phillip would die, but at the same time, he felt a sense of peace and release. John remained committed to follow God's will.

When he returned home, John told Vera Mae, "I've committed Phillip into the Lord's keeping."

A few weeks later, the Perkinses were able to take Phillip to an excellent doctor in Louisiana. "He's got polio," the doctor told them.

That night, the Perkinses got on their knees and prayed together, "Lord, please don't take Phillip, but raise him up." Later that summer, they took Phillip to a special children's hospital in California that confirmed Phillip's diagnosis. "But he's already begun to heal," they said. Within a year, Phillip was fully recovered.

Even facing the uncertainty and fear caused by having a child with polio, John Perkins remained convinced that he must follow God's call.

16

Voter Registration

Wherever he went, John pursued opportunities for reaching people with the Good News. While registering his children for public school in 1960, John was invited to teach a Bible class. Soon he began teaching in seven different Mississippi counties.

In early spring 1961, John and his family moved to the nearby town of Mendenhall. Here they established a home base for their work with the youth. They called their little storefront mission Fisherman's Mission.

In addition to leading kids to Christ, John and Vera began to minister to the community's physical needs as well, and as the ministry grew, John changed its name to

Voice of Calvary Ministries. He started an after-school tutoring program for children who had fallen behind in their education. The housing needs of the black community prompted the Voice of Calvary to build duplex homes and rent them at low rates. For the youth, the group built a playground and then a gym for recreation. To encourage good nutrition and health among children and their parents, the Voice of Calvary started a cooperative food store. Eventually, they even developed a cooperative farm to provide fresh produce for the store.

But these improvements were short-term helps for a black community that was controlled by white marshals and elected officials. John knew that the best way to ensure long-term help for the black community was to encourage voting among blacks. But in the early sixties, few blacks could afford the state's voting tax. And those who could afford it were often kept away from the polls by white sheriffs.

Others were held back by literacy or reading tests at voter registration desks. At registration, potential voters had to fill out long questionnaires about family history. Next, they had to read a section of the state constitution and write an explanation of it. White voter registrars judged the results. Some never allowed blacks to pass the test.

Without the power to vote in elections, Mississippi blacks had no opportunity to influence or remove from office white sheriffs or other officials who ignored their needs.

With several other leaders in the black community, John soon organized black voter registration drives. John became representative for all of Simpson and Lawrence Counties and for parts of Rankin and Smith Counties, and he spread the word about voter registration through the best network possible — the church.

In churches across Mississippi, church members would stand and announce, "John Perkins from the Voice of Calvary has been appointed the representative for our county. You can now register to vote out behind the post office." Although most of the people were afraid, the chance to vote was what many blacks had been waiting for. They formed long lines to register.

The Voice of Calvary helped with registration by using a school bus to transport residents from the rural areas of Mississippi. The bus had been purchased to transport kids to Bible classes. That summer, over one thousand blacks registered to vote. In Simpson county where John lived, only fifty voters had registered the previous year!

With so many blacks voting, many whites became concerned that they would lose power. And that is exactly what began to happen. In 1968, for instance, a former school teacher named William "Shag" Pyron ran against Southern District Commissioner John D. Smith, a man outspoken against blacks. In his twenty

years in office, not one black had worked for the highway department in his area of the state. "It's about time
that blacks work for the highway department," Pyron
told black leaders during his campaign. "If I get elected, I'll see that it happens."

The black community supported Pyron. He won
the race for commissioner of the southern district. For
the first time in the Mendenhall area, blacks had exer-
cised their power in the voting booths. And, once
again, John became known as a troublemaker. He
became the target of the white community's threats.

"Perkins is a troublemaker," said one caller. "He
could get himself killed." CLICK.

"Mrs. Perkins, you don't want to be a widow, do
you?" CLICK.

"Reverend Perkins is as good as dead right now.
You'd better get out of town fast." CLICK.

John took these threats seriously, and he worried
about the safety of Vera Mae and his children, especially
when he traveled out of town to speak at conferences or
conventions. After all, black churches had been bombed
and black activitists murdered throughout Mississippi.

Early one morning when John was away, Vera Mae
thought she heard someone in the front of the house.
She got out of bed and turned on a light. Instantly, a
car squealed away, spraying gravel down the street. As
Vera Mae reached the bedroom window, she saw an old
pickup truck turn the corner. Instinctively, she knew

that the truck had been parked alongside her family's car, perhaps in an attempt to plant a bomb inside it.

She called the police and reported her suspicion. "Someone will be right there to investigate, Mrs. Perkins," the officer assured her on the phone. A patrol car should have reached the house in less than five minutes. But Vera Mae waited and waited. A half hour. An hour. Then she called the Federal Bureau of Investigation in Jackson. They promised to send someone right away and cautioned her not to touch the car until an agent arrived.

Vera Mae borrowed a car to take her children to school and then waited for the FBI agent. He arrived about nine o'clock. From a safe distance, Vera Mae watched the agent crawl under the car and examine it. Then he gently opened the car door and looked under the dashboard. Finally he looked inside the engine. Nothing.

Visibly relieved, the agent said, "It looks as if your car is safe. Apparently you surprised the men before they could plant a bomb."

After this incident, cars began to appear near the Perkins's house during the night. When John looked out into the cars, he saw white men, armed and waiting. These men watched the Perkins's house for hours, slowly moving closer. They seemed to be waiting for just the right occasion to attack.

Finally, one Sunday afternoon, John went to seek

advice from his community. By eight in the evening, his church was packed with people.

"We've got to do something to help you, John," one of the church elders said. "You've done so much for us. Now we need to protect you," another man said.

That night they formed a volunteer group to take up weapons and guard the Perkins's home. Silent in the blanket of darkness, these men waited, watched, and listened, hoping and praying that dawn would come without anything happening.

To their relief, the cars disappeared. John's enemies had kept their silent watch only when there was no possibility of open warfare. They had not wanted violence — only control. The election passed without incident, and the Perkins family breathed a collective sigh of relief.

As the blacks' movement for civil rights grew in intensity, black leaders met at the Perkins's home several times a week. The Perkins children listened to their long discussions.

In the fall of 1966, all five of the Perkins children enrolled, along with six other black children, in what had been all-white public schools. Earlier that fall, a preacher had spoken to the students about accepting Christ. And, although a number of white students publicly accepted Christ as their Savior, their new faith didn't affect their relationships with the black students. For two years, Spencer and Joanie walked alone through the halls of the high school. No white student would sit down with them or talk with them.

For two years, John felt his children's pain as they endured this prejudice. It became unbearable. He could no longer bear to watch them suffer, so he removed them and sent them to black schools. He wished the Good News about Jesus could bridge racial barriers. *Where is God's love and concern for my children?* he wondered.

Although the pressure had been too much for the children, John continued to work for love between the races and social justice for the black community. Slowly, the winds of change began to blow.

17

Arrested!

Racial tension in the South continued to rise. Martin Luther King Jr., the civil rights leader, had been assassinated. The nightly news flashed pictures of blacks marching and protesting across the South.

In Mendenhall, John Perkins was right in the middle of all this tension. Outside the town, a billboard on Highway 49 read, "White people unite. Defeat Jew/Communist race mixers." It was designed to unify white people against all of the racial integration throughout the South — especially in Mississippi.

John knew that not all white people opposed the Civil Rights Movement. One of them was Doug

Huemmer, a college student who had come to
Mendenhall to work alongside John in the ministry at
the Voice of Calvary. Doug quickly earned a reputation
as a hard-working volunteer.

Now, several days before Christmas, Doug and
John drove to a small country grocery store where he
could buy a bottle of cane syrup, a taste of the South
for his parents' Christmas gift.

The sun was beginning to set as they walked into
the store. Immediately they heard some loud talking. A
young black man, Garland Wilks, was in a heated dis-
cussion with the white store clerk. Garland was yelling,
angry at the clerk for not accepting his check for a few
items. Although Garland wasn't drunk, John could tell
that he had been drinking. From John's longtime experience with the local police, he knew it wouldn't be long
before they came to rough up this "drunk nigger." To
prevent that, John decided to step in and help.

"Garland," John asked, "could we give you a ride
home?"

At first, Garland didn't want to go, but John insisted. "Come on, you don't need these things. Let's go."

To John's surprise, Garland let the two men guide
him outside and into the backseat of the car. Both men
felt relieved that they had prevented trouble.

Unfortunately, the store clerk had already called
the police. He was angry about Garland's attitude and
wanted the young man arrested.

"Uh-oh," Doug said as he looked in his rearview mirror. John turned around in his seat. A local police car followed right behind. John began to feel nervous, but thought, *They're not going to stop us. They don't have their lights turned on.*

As if reading his mind, the car lights flashed on. Doug immediately pulled off to the side of the road. He and John got out of the car and walked toward the police car.

"What's wrong, officer?" Doug asked.

Two policemen got out of the car. "You just shut up!" one yelled at Doug. "Stand aside!"

The other officer stuck his head inside Doug's car. "You come out of that car, Garland. You're under arrest."

John looked surprised and asked, "Under arrest? For what?"

"For drunkenness and disturbing the peace," the officer growled.

"But he's just sitting in our car and not disturbing the peace," John said.

"You just shut up!" the policeman shouted.

John had no intention of making the policeman angry. From others in the black community, John had heard many stories about the police beating blacks. While John didn't believe all the stories, he had seen enough bruises and scars for himself to believe some of them. He knew that many employees in Mississippi's sheriff and police departments sympathized with the

Ku Klux Klan, a group known for its violence against blacks.

Doug and John watched helplessly as Garland was pushed into the backseat of the patrol car. After the car drove away, Doug and John went to the Berean Bible Church where a group of high school and college students were practicing for their Christmas pageant.

The students were already upset about another arrest earlier in the day.

"Roy Berry was arrested and beaten," one of the students said. "Supposedly he had been calling a white woman and asking her for a date."

"Reverend Perkins, they beat him real bad," one of the women sobbed. "They told him that they ought to kill him. And now they're gonna beat up Garland, too."

John knew the girl was probably right, but what could he do? He knew that if he went to the station, the police would probably arrest and beat him, too.

Then he had a clever thought. "What if we all went? They couldn't arrest everyone!"

After discussing it, seventeen people, including four of the Perkins children, hurried to the Mendenhall City Hall.

In the parking lot, Mark Sherman, the chief of police, met the Voice of Calvary group and reported that Garland was being treated well.

"But what about Roy Berry?" someone asked. "He was beat up."

The police chief quickly explained that his department had nothing to do with Berry's arrest. "That case was handled by the county sheriff's department, and if you'd like to find out about it, then you need to go to the county jail," he said.

As the group crowded into the front entrance of the county jail, John announced, "We've come to see Roy Berry."

About a dozen people followed the jailer as he led them into the booking room. "We want to see Roy Berry," John repeated.

They were shocked by the jailer's response.

"You're all under arrest," he said, opening the large steel doors to the holding cell. Doug stood in front of John, so the jailer grabbed him and pushed him inside. John and his group followed.

SLAM. As the door shut, the jailer repeated, "You're all under arrest."

"What's the charge?" someone asked.

"We just came to see our friend," another person chimed.

"I'm going to smother in here!" someone yelled.

"I can't breathe," said another.

To keep things from getting out of control, the jailer called for reinforcements. Within a few minutes, the sheriff, district attorney, and several officers from the Mississippi State Highway Patrol arrived. They huddled in a corner planning what to do with the group.

Like wildfire, the news of the arrest spread throughout the town. A crowd of family and friends quickly gathered outside the jail. Through the small cell window, John could see Vera Mae among his friends.

A mean-looking officer approached the door of the cell. "Tell you what, kids. If you leave nice and easy, nobody will be hurt. We just want to keep Reverend Perkins and this Huemmer fella overnight. But you kids better get out of here."

The kids didn't believe that no harm would come to their leaders. One of them spoke up for the group. If John wasn't allowed to leave, none of them would leave. Everyone nodded in agreement.

The policeman cursed under his breath, shook his head, and walked back over to the group of whispering officials. They would have to try something else.

The crowd outside the jail continued to grow. By now, over 100 people had gathered. John and the others could hear their angry voices demanding to know what was happening.

Then John heard the distinct voice of a highway patrolman named Lloyd "Goon" Jones. "You folks better go home peacefully," Goon said to the crowd. "John Perkins is a false leader who gets you people into all sorts of trouble." No one budged. Although John appreciated the support of his family and friends, he began to worry that violence might erupt. What about the kids with him? And his family? He didn't want anyone to get hurt.

Moving over to the small window in the second-story cell, John called to the people gathered below. After getting their attention, he told them how much he appreciated their support and love. "But be careful," he warned. "I know you're angry. I know you feel like getting back at them, but we can't do that."

John urged the people not to resort to violence but encouraged them to stand firm against injustice. "If someone has to suffer," John said, "I'm willing for it to be me. I'm willing to die if that is what has to happen."

Suddenly, John had an idea. It was almost Christmas, the perfect time for an economic boycott. John encouraged the crowd to shop somewhere other than in Mendenhall. He knew that many had put their Christmas purchases on layaway plans to allow gradual payment and pick-up just before the holiday. There was still time to cancel those purchases! An economic boycott would let the white store owners in the town know how the blacks felt about their unjust treatment.

The crowd cheered John's idea, but the officers thought John had talked long enough. They announced that John and Doug were under arrest and that everyone else must go.

"If the kids don't go on their own, then we will force them to go," the officer threatened. The teenagers didn't change their mind about staying. So, one by one, the officials carried them out of the jail cell. Soon only Doug and John were left.

Doug had missed his flight home to California for the Christmas holidays. John looked at Doug with sad eyes, worried that he'd be unable to get another flight during the busy travel period. But Doug wasn't concerned. He felt that helping John and the ministry was the most important action he could take.

About two or three in the morning, the two men were charged with their crime and moved into another cell. Outside the jail, most of the supporters drifted off to their homes. Vera Mae and some others went to the Voice of Calvary to organize the economic boycott. They made signs to picket the stores the next day and to spread the word throughout the black community.

Most people decided that the sacrifice of convenient Christmas shopping was worth the cost. With just two days to prepare for Christmas, the streets of Mendenhall were nearly empty. Even the white shoppers didn't want to appear, afraid to confront the protesters who carried their signs in front of the shops.

The shop owners were desperate to end the boycott. They pressured the police to release John and Doug.

After one night in jail, an officer came to their cell and said nicely, "Why don't you just post bail and be with your family for Christmas? I hate to see you here for the holidays." John sensed a difference in the man. Why hadn't he suggested this action the night before?

"If the sheriff wants Doug and me out of jail, he should drop the charges against us," John said.

But dropping the charges would be a confession that Doug and John had done nothing wrong in the first place. The officer refused. Doug and John said they would have to think for awhile. For the rest of the afternoon they sat behind bars. When they realized that the charges would not be dropped, they posted the necessary money for bail and were released. At the same time, Garland Wilks and Roy Berry were also released.

*   *   *

Back at the Voice of Calvary, John's supporters prayed and decided to continue the boycott until city officials met four demands: First, all charges against John and Doug must be dropped. Second, the city must repair the streets in the black section of town. Third, the police must make fair arrests consistent with the United States Constitution. Finally, a representative number of blacks must be employed in Mendenhall businesses.

John and the others didn't think these demands were unreasonable, but the Mendenhall officials told them, "We won't even consider them."

The black community felt that it had no choice but to continue the boycott until its concerns were given the proper attention.

Every Saturday during January and February, a

parade of blacks marched from the Voice of Calvary, through the city streets to the City Hall, and then back to the starting point. Hundreds marched and chanted, "Do right, white man. Do right!" All along the parade route, dozens of heavily armed, white highway patrolmen and police stood watching with angry looks. But the marchers were careful not to provoke the police or do anything to incite violence.

During these months of protest, the white community waited, believing that the black community would simply run out of steam and end the boycott. Instead, the number of marchers increased every week. Many blacks came to march from other communities, including some students from Tougaloo College in Jackson.

At one point, the desperate store owners tried to bribe one of the local black leaders. They offered him $2,000 to convince residents not to boycott. Although he took their money and tried to convince the protesters, no one listened to him. The store owners had wasted their money.

The white community grew desperate.

18

Beaten

On Saturday, February 7, John marched with the others, including a large group from Tougaloo College. The protest was exciting and encouraging to John. After the march, the group met at the Voice of Calvary to praise God for the successful protest and to make plans for the following Saturday. The meeting broke up late in the afternoon.

About 7:30 P.M., the Perkins's telephone rang. Through tears, a woman told John, "The highway patrol stopped Doug Huemmer's bus, arrested him, and carried nineteen college students off to the Brandon jail."

Vera Mae could tell something was wrong. "What is it?" she demanded when John hung up the phone.

"The college students have been stopped by the highway patrol."

"Well?" Vera Mae hoped they had gotten a speeding ticket or something simple.

"The kids that were with Doug have been arrested, and they're in the jail at Brandon," John said.

"Brandon! Oh, no!" Both Vera Mae and John knew the reputation of Jonathan Edwards, the sheriff in Brandon. He was well known for his antiblack opinions.

John remembered seeing the sheriff's son on the sidelines during their march that afternoon. He had stood beside "Goon" Jones, the officer involved in John's arrest in Mendenhall.

"What are you going to do?" Vera Mae asked, but she already knew the answer.

John shrugged. "The only thing I know to do — go up there and see what's going on, try to get those kids out of jail."

Vera Mae frowned but didn't try to stop her husband. "You be careful," she said.

John invited Curry Brown and Joe Paul Buckley, two friends from the boycott, to go with him to Brandon. He knew that he could use the support and the company. It was a forty-five minute drive. Although John worried he might be stopped on the way, he never expected what awaited him in Brandon.

At the courthouse, a uniformed patrolman greeted the men and told them where to park. He was friendly — almost too friendly. When they asked to see the sheriff, he said, "You stay here. I'll go tell him that you're here."

The three men stood outside their car, quietly waiting for the sheriff. He never came. Instead, more than a dozen patrolmen arrived. "You're all under arrest," one said, beginning a search of the men and their car. Then the officers herded the men toward the jail. Along the way, they began to beat them. One patrolman kicked Curry's back and side and then punched him in the head.*

Once inside the jail, more white police gathered around. All were anxious to throw a punch or swing their leather clubs. *They're going to kill us all,* John thought, seeing the hatred on each face. *And they want us to suffer first.*

"You think you're one smart nigger!" Sheriff Edwards yelled, just inches from John's face. "Well, you ain't in Simpson County anymore. We know how to treat smart niggers here in Rankin County."

The sheriff hit John with his fists as he talked. "This is a whole new ball game, nigger! How do you like this, nigger?"

_____

*This and the account that follows is based on testimony given by John and other witnesses in court proceedings following the arrests.

John resisted the urge to defend himself. If he fought back, they would kill him right away. John raised his hands to ward off the blows, but strong policemen surrounded him. They struck from the front, the back, and the side. Nothing could protect him. Half-conscious, John fell to his knees on the floor. *Maybe it will stop,* he thought. It didn't. Now the men kicked him in the back, the head, and the groin. Finally, he passed out.

When John stirred, the men attacked again. Over and over they struck. The pain was terrible. John's blood sprayed across the floor.

But John wasn't the only victim. The police brutalized Curry, Joe Paul, and the college students, as well. Some time during the night, they even shaved Doug Huemmer's head and beard and poured whiskey all over him. They did the same to Curry.

Between blows, John saw the men drinking from paper cups. He recognized the smell — homemade moonshine. The more they drank, the more violent they became.

Later in the night, the men started to scream at John for bleeding on the floor. "Hey, nigger," one of them said, "what are you doing bleeding all over my floor? Hey, Ralph, you see what this nigger has done to our floor?"

"Why, that's disgusting," the other man said. "You just get up right now and clean up this mess!"

The men threw a mop and bucket on the floor and forced John to start cleaning. John doubled over in pain and felt as if he would pass out any minute. The men continued to hit and slap him, all the while complaining about his work.

"Best get this mess cleaned up," John heard one of them say to another. "The feds will be here shortly." All evidence of the beatings had to be gone before the FBI arrived on the scene. Unfortunately for John and his friends, they never came. The police grew even more violent and angry.

One of them pulled out his gun and pressed it against John's head. "I think I'm gonna kill me a nigger!" The steel was cold against John's head.

This is it, he thought. Slowly the man squeezed the trigger. CLICK. The chamber in the pistol had been empty. The room echoed with laughter as the beating resumed. Finally, John slipped into the darkness of unconsciousness.

When he regained consciousness, John saw that the men had created another game. Someone had brought in Mendenhall's four boycott demands. The officers ordered John to read the list. He could barely see anything. As John read aloud, the officers met each point with blows. John's throat was so sore that he could barely read above a whisper.

"Nigger, read louder!" they demanded.

"I just hate a nigger who won't speak up," someone else said with a laugh.

John lost track of the time. Though it was almost
impossible, he tried to focus his attention on Jesus
Christ. He took comfort in knowing that Jesus had had
to face beating and suffering, too.

Finally, after hours of beatings, the men quit.
Each man was booked, fingerprinted, and taken
upstairs to a cell.*

*   *   *

John lay on his bed. Although every part of his
body ached, he felt pity for the men who had beaten
him. Hate had turned these men into savages.
Recalling their faces, John felt cold shivers through his
body, but he was determined not to let their hatred
destroy his relationship with Christ. He would not hate
them back. Instead he focused on the love of God and
asked God to fill his heart with love.

Sunday morning, a guard came to John's cell.
"You have a visitor," he announced, unlocking the cell
and leading John to a small room. There sat Vera Mae.
John knew that he didn't look good. But he also knew
that Vera Mae couldn't let on about his condition. A
policeman stood watching and listening to every move.

_____

*In later court proceedings, Sheriff Edwards testified he struck
John only two or three times after John swung at him, and that a general
"fracas" broke out in the jail.

Standing, Vera Mae wrapped her arms around John and whispered, "What happened to you?"

John leaned into her shoulder and said, "Get me out of here. They're gonna kill me first."

It took a lot of money to release the twenty-three people in the Brandon jail. Friends of the Voice of Calvary helped, and by Sunday afternoon John was free. But there wasn't enough money for everyone until Monday afternoon, and throughout his last night in jail, Curry Brown heard the jailer taunting, "All your friends have forgotten you. They have left you here to rot in jail."

One by one, the prisoners went to the home of Luvell Purvis, a friend who treated their wounds and offered what comfort he could. John was still resting in the Purvis home when Curry arrived. The two men held each other and cried.

John led one final march the very next Saturday. But this time the marchers were blocked by National Guardsmen and state troopers all sporting riot gear and shotguns. The white community had made it clear that they would go to any length to keep blacks from demanding their rights. The blacks stopped marching, but they continued their boycott until most of their demands were met.

A few months later, John was tried in Mendenhall. He was accused of contributing to the delinquency of minors. Many of his friends crowded into the courtroom. But the trial was set to go against John from the beginning. The judge was against John. When John's youngest baby began to cry during the proceedings, the judge pounded his gavel and yelled, "Shut that kid up or I'll throw all you niggers out of court." Later when John testified, he allowed jokes and hoots from the whites in the audience and even smiled and laughed as John described his torture.

The stress of the trial began to wear on John's nerves. Falsely accused of many crimes during the trial, John felt broken. Friends who lined the balcony of the courtroom saw the tension and sadness in their leader's face. His head sunk and his mouth quivered. *How can I possibly challenge these false charges before a white judge and all-white jury? Can there possibly be justice?* John wondered. *And what of the people who were counting on my leadership? If I can't stand up to this injustice, how can I guide others to fight?*

"This court will be recessed for a thirty minute break," the judge said, pounding his gavel and retreating to his private chambers. John slipped out the back and headed to the drinking fountain. After a long drink, John looked up into the face of a stern black woman in a floppy hat. Her face blazed with anger, and her eyes seemed to burn right into John. "Son, stand up! Stand up!"

John threw back his shoulders, sucked in his stomach, and smiled for the first time in days. He marched back into the courtroom, determined to fight for his people.

The legal battle continued for almost two years. Finally, the officials agreed to drop all charges against John. In exchange, John agreed to drop his suit against the state of Mississippi.

During the next year and a half, John suffered still more. After almost recovering from his jail wounds, John was stricken with high blood pressure and irregularities in his heart. Then, while on a speaking trip in Ann Arbor, Michigan, John bent over double. His stomach hurt with cramps. Once he returned to Mississippi, doctors discovered severe ulcers in his stomach. They operated immediately and removed two thirds of John's stomach. His weight dropped from 170 to 140 pounds.

Recovering from the surgery in Mount Bayou, Mississippi, John thought about the Brandon jail beatings. Fear tore at his mind. It didn't look as if there would be justice in Mississippi.

From personal experience, John knew the power of the Gospel of Jesus Christ. He believed it could break the hatred in Mississippi. But, sadly, he had not seen that happen. Only occasionally had someone broken through the barriers.

But then John remembered the early days of his ministry, the blacks who had flocked to the voting booths, the radio program he'd started, and the tent meetings where he'd preached the Good News about Jesus. People had responded.

He considered the white brothers and sisters in California who faithfully sent money and other resources to support the work at the Voice of Calvary. He thought of the white doctors who treated him in Michigan and the students like Doug Huemmer who were working for just $100 per month.

Although the bruises and scars from his beating were still tender, John reached two critical decisions as he lay in bed. First, he would not fill his life with hatred. *Love has greater power than hate,* John thought. *There is no power in violence, but only in the hope of Jesus Christ filling our lives with love.* Through the pain of his bruises, John knew that God had washed away his hate and filled him with a love for white people. Second, he would not try to be a hero anymore. *I can't be a black superman leading people to the Promised Land,* he thought. *I can't lead everything alone. Only through a sense of community can lives be changed.*

As John prayed about his future, painful memories faded. Hope filled his heart, and John saw a new beginning for his ministry.

19

Flood!

There was still plenty of work to be done. People — both black and white — needed Christ. And the blacks needed better education, working opportunities, and health care. *I've got to train leaders,* John thought over and over as he worked in the Mendenhall area.

One Sunday, the Perkins family was driving into Mendenhall after John had preached. While the kids slept in the back of the station wagon, John talked with Vera Mae. "God's been preparing me to develop leaders in our community. I can help others gain practical experience in ministry."

His words hit Vera Mae like a ton of bricks. *I'll be*

stuck here in Mendenhall forever, she thought. *It will take ten to twelve years to train leaders to take our place.*

"I'll never have a nice house again," she blurted out.

During his time in Christian ministry, John had watched various leaders neglect family life. He was determined not to be like them. But John knew that God had brought them to Mississippi, and he was determined to stay and train others to continue his work. An opportunity soon arose.

One day, Dolphus Weary, a poor young black man, went to the Mendenhall barber shop. As Leonard Stapleton cut his hair, the two men talked. "Are you a Christian?" Leonard asked.

"I guess so," Dolphus said. "I go to church and do right, and I've been baptized and all of that."

"But you still aren't sure if you are a Christian?" Leonard persisted. He suggested that Dolphus attend one of the tent meetings where John Perkins was preaching.

That night as Dolphus sat in the audience, John preached on Psalm 116:12: "How can I repay the Lord for all his goodness to me?" Dolphus considered his life and his past sins. He knew he must give his life to Christ. He began to spend time at the Voice of Calvary with John.

The two worked side by side, tutoring children,

starting a radio show and food program, and building a gym for neighborhood kids. "Don't limit your dreams with your resources," John always insisted. "Dream far beyond what you have."

It was John who taught Dolphus about life in Christ. Whenever the church doors were open for a youth ministry, Dolphus was there. As John modeled the Christian life, Dolphus grew in his faith and abilities.

John can see opportunities where there doesn't appear to be any, Dolphus thought. *He can rise above a situation and see a creative solution.* Over and over, Dolphus watched John move ahead in faith, taking risks without fear.

One day Dolphus came to John. "I've got an opportunity for work in California," Dolphus said. "It's a great possibility, but I'm unsure what God wants."

John stretched his arm across the young man's shoulders. "We need you here, Dolphus. You're a critical part of what God is doing through the Voice of Calvary." With John's encouragement, Dolphus decided to let the other opportunity pass and stay and help John with his ministry.

The two men's first challenge was to improve the medical treatment available for blacks. A survey showed that 85 percent of Mendenhall's black community had never seen a doctor. The reasons were many. The only doctors in Simpson County were white. The ones who would treat blacks had separate waiting rooms for whites and blacks and would treat all white patients first. Sometimes patients waited all day and still received no medical attention.

In 1973, John and Dolphus started a health clinic headed by Dr. Kevin Lake from Pasadena. Dr. Lake stayed several months before turning over the work to two other doctors. But the clinic's success was short-lived. Later that year, the clinic was without a doctor. John, Dolphus, and Vera Mae searched and searched for a permanent doctor, but none could be found.

Then, on the eve of a dedication service for an expensive x-ray machine, disaster struck. Torrential rains threatened the low-lying sections of town, including the site of the Voice of Calvary. In knee-deep water, Dolphus Weary and the ministry staff worked frantically to move the clinic's equipment to high ground. A record-breaking fifteen inches of rain fell in just thirty hours.

John and Dolphus stood on the railroad embankment watching the waters stream through the doors and windows of their houses. As they walked toward the railroad bridge, they heard someone shout, "Look at the house! It's floating this way!" The two men watched in fascination as a home broke from its foundation. It rocked like a ship, caught on fire for a moment, then crashed into another home already stuck under the bridge.

John and Dolphus watched helplessly as rain

water swept through the Voice of Calvary property —
its chapel, tutorial school, gym, co-op store, and
homes. John couldn't reconcile this disaster with the
promise of Romans 8:28, "In everything God works
together for good." He felt as if his life's work was
being swept away by the flood.

Just a few months earlier, John and Vera Mae had
moved to Jackson to start a new ministry. Now they were
back in Mendenhall helping Dolphus with this crisis.

The damage was extensive and the community
discouraged. The Voice of Calvary staff met to pray for
the community and ask, "What next?"

"This flood gives us the same challenge we've
faced for fourteen years," John told his staff. "We must
identify needs, trust in the Lord, and fill those needs in
the name of Jesus."

Late into the night, the black community met at
one of the few buildings that remained on the property at the Voice of Calvary. John opened the meeting
with prayer: "Father, help us to have a sense of your
presence and unity as we meet together. We need your
wisdom and your insight for this disaster."

The group formed the Community Disaster
Committee and elected Dolphus Weary as its chair-
man. At the end of the meeting, someone got up and
said, "You know, this is the first time I can remember
that the people of Mendenhall have gotten together as
a community."

In just twenty-four hours — even before the Red Cross had arrived — the committee had surveyed the area and made a plan. They involved Mendenhall's white leaders and asked Mayor Ray Layton to represent their needs to the governor of Mississippi. They worked together to clean up as the waters receded.

Slowly, the damage was repaired, but the black community still needed a doctor for its clinic. In October of 1974, Dr. Eugene McCarty, a young pediatrician from Colorado Springs, Colorado, visited Mendenhall with his wife, Joanne. For several evenings, John and Dr. McCarty talked late into the night. Then during the Sunday morning church service, the soft-spoken doctor rose. "My wife and I are convicted by what the Lord is doing here," Dr. McCarty said. "We want to become part of your ministry if you will have us."

The people in the service began to shout praises to God. Some even cried. Dr. McCarty was an answer to prayer. Now the community would have reliable, affordable health care. But more than that, John, Vera Mae, and the rest of the staff had new hope that others would join their ministry.

While John and Vera Mae moved to Jackson, Mississippi and expanded the work of the Voice of Calvary, Dolphus Weary stayed in Mendenhall as the director of the Mendenhall Ministries. The dream of new leadership and an expanded ministry was coming true.

20

Harambee

Now announcing the arrival of Flight 1584 from Boston," the airport speaker blared. With his well-worn travel bag, John stepped out of the airplane and greeted Vera Mae in Jackson. Airplanes, conferences, and church meetings across the country were now part of John's daily routine.

John had spent ten years building the Jackson ministry. Lem Tucker, the director of the Jackson ministry, had taken on the day-to-day decisionmaking. John had just a few days at home between trips to hear about Lem's decisions and to give him advice. But John was confident in Lem's leadership. *Lem does a better job than I would do,* John thought, hearing about the thoughtful way Lem handled whatever problems arose. *I'm glad there are some outstanding leaders in our ministry.*

One night in a motel near Wichita, Kansas, John awoke from a sound sleep. He turned on the light and reached for his tape recorder. "With this letter, I am officially resigning from the Voice of Calvary Ministries in Jackson, Mississippi," he said into the microphone. "I've decided that my time is up. I don't want to mess up all that I have achieved." He was deliberate and sure. He recognized the growing leadership of men like Lem Tucker, Phil Reed, and his son Spencer Perkins.

The national board of the Voice of Calvary selected a committee to help John relocate. He wanted to move far enough away to resist the temptation to interfere with the work in Jackson and Mendenhall, Mississippi. After two meetings, the committee suggested a number of places to relocate, but said, "It really doesn't matter where you want to be if helping other ministries is going to be your task."

The committee members turned to Vera Mae and asked, "Where would you like to live?"

"I'd like to live in California," she said without hesitation. And it wasn't long before John and Vera Mae found a place for ministry there.

*   *   *

"In Northwest Pasadena, another person fell victim

to a drive-by shooting," the newscaster announced. "It's just one more of a series of crimes in this area." Over and over, the northwest part of Pasadena drew John and Vera Mae's attention. The section was known for drug operations and the highest daytime crime rate in Southern California.

One afternoon, John was driving in the Pasadena area with his friend Paul Gibson. "Look at that empty house over there," John said as they drove past. Later that afternoon the two men stopped at Lake Avenue Congregational Church in Pasadena, a church the Perkinses often attended. One of the men in the church knew about this empty home. He brought John and Vera Mae to look inside.

The home was broken down and needed repair. With well-developed construction skills, John was prepared to do the work, but Vera Mae was hesitant.

"Tupey, I don't like it," she said. "It's too run-down." As they stepped outside, John and Vera Mae noticed another house across the street. Its sign read "for sale by owner." Saying goodbye to their realtor friend, the Perkins circled the block and returned to the house. A ninety-two-year-old grandmother answered the door. For over two years she had tried to sell. But because her own grandson sold drugs from the home, the police had raided the place over and over again, making it impossible to attract buyers.

John and Vera Mae pitied the woman and knew they had found a home.

Almost immediately the Perkinses were thrown into the neighborhood conflict. Their neighbors operated one of the largest drug houses in the area. Often, twenty to thirty cars an hour arrived to purchase drugs. Occasionally, an ambulance would pull in front of the house, and John and Vera Mae would see the horrible results of drug-related violence.

Twice, fire engines roared to the Perkins's house. Afraid that the Perkins were cutting into their drug traffic and money, the drug dealers set fire to their home. Later, they even threw bombs. Luckily, John, Vera Mae, and the children were spared each time. And, rather than discourage the Perkinses, these scares reminded them of their mission. Each incident strengthened their determination to fight for the lives of their neighbors.

John and Vera Mae soon began neighborhood Bible studies and prayer meetings. A Good News Club for children met in their garage. It was a safe place for neighborhood children to learn about Jesus. That in place, the Perkinses opened a center for children.

The neighborhood ministry was underway, and further expansion was just around the corner — or around the world.

* * *

One day in 1980, John and his two sons, Spencer

and Derek, traveled to Kenya, Africa. Standing in the shadow of Kilimanjaro, the Perkinses watched the hurried activity of hundreds of people. In a single day, they were building a school. They called it a "Harambee," which means, "Let's get together and push" or "Let's pull together."

People from miles around the area came to participate, even the president of Kenya. Each brought something of value to be auctioned, such as a pig, a duck, or a goat. "Who will give me seven dollars?" cried the auctioneer. Someone waved.

"Okay, how about seven fifty?" the auctioneer continued. Finally, the pig sold for twenty dollars. One item at a time, the community raised about $30,000 to purchase materials for a new school. John was inspired by their achievement. He knew he must take the Harambee concept back to northwest Pasadena.

Several years later, a reporter from the *Los Angeles Times* followed John around his Harambee Christian Center in Pasadena. At the end of the day, he pulled out his pad and asked, "John, what are you doing here?"

John answered without pause, "We're trying to meet the greatest need in this community: care for the children. I want the kids to be able to play in the street again," he said, gesturing outside where drive-by shootings threatened kids at play.

Slowly, the Harambee Christian Family Center

took over a neighborhood in Pasadena, occupying two, then three, four, five houses. Mrs. Jackson, one of its volunteers, expanded its ministry by reaching out to ex-prisoners. She saw that many released prisoners returned to crime and went back into prison. To help released prisoners rejoin society, she opened homes where they could live and started a church where they could worship.

Two houses became a day camp and after-school center for ninety children. "I pledge allegiance to the Christian flag," they chanted, led by college students who volunteered time to teach reading, writing, and Bible stories, and to organize hikes and skits. Every now and then, John would walk out into the halls just to listen. The sound of children learning in safety was music to his ears.

21

A Dream That Lasts

In the spring of 1980, John Perkins sorted through his mail. A return address caught his eye: "President's Office, Wheaton College, Wheaton, Illinois." Tearing open the letter, John read with delight, "We'd like to present you with an honorary doctorate degree from Wheaton College at our graduation ceremonies this May. Will you accept such a degree?"

"Vera Mae. Vera Mae!" John shouted. "Come look at this letter!"

Later that spring, John wore the traditional cap and gown and accepted the honorary degree, a degree which opened another world of opportunity for him. Shortly after, Oxford University in England asked John to teach some courses as a visiting instructor. Over the next fourteen years, John received three additional doctorates, and Vera Mae received one.

But John's influence wasn't limited to the academic world. In 1994, President Bill Clinton invited John to the Oval Office for a White House briefing. He was one of a dozen religious leaders — Catholic, Mormon, and Protestant — to attend the session. It wasn't John's first visit to the White House. Presidents such as Jimmy Carter and Ronald Reagan had previously asked John to serve on advisory committees.

John's ministry had expanded far past the black community of Mendenhall, Mississippi. But such success did not signal quitting time for John. In the past ten years, John has been busy telling people of God's love and encouraging them to demonstrate this love to the poor. Meanwhile, he has established some organizations and publications that will keep his message alive long after he is gone.

In 1989 he organized the Christian Community Development Association. It has quickly grown to over three hundred national ministries who follow John's method of ministry. He has also started two magazines with his oldest son, Spencer. *Urban Family* is a magazine of hope for inner city families, and *The Reconciler* is a magazine whose mission is to unite the body of Christ across racial lines.

In the fall of 1995, John embarked on yet another journey of service by starting the Harambee Preparatory School in northwest Pasadena. The school opened with twenty-one students from kindergarten to third grade. Through this school, John hoped to give poor children a solid education so they could go on to achieve great deeds.

Whether he's at the White House or in his own neighborhood, whether he's teaching young children or preaching to adults, John Perkins has lived out his dream — to reach across racial lines and see people as God sees them, with the love of Jesus Christ.